# Past Perfect

# Past Perfect

Michel Tremblay

translated by
Linda Gaboriau

Talonbooks
2004

Copyright © 2004 Michel Tremblay
Translation copyright © 2004 Linda Gaboriau

Talonbooks
P.O. Box 2076, Vancouver, British Columbia, Canada V6B 3S3
www.talonbooks.com

Typeset in New Baskerville and printed and bound in Canada on 100%
post-consumer recycled paper.

Second Printing: April 2007

The publisher gratefully acknowledges the financial support of the
Canada Council for the Arts; the Government of Canada through the
Book Publishing Industry Development Program; and the Province of
British Columbia through the British Columbia Arts Council for our
publishing activities.

*Le Passé antérieur* was published in the original French by Leméac
Éditeur, Montréal, Québec in 2003.

**National Library of Canada Cataloguing in Publication Data**
Tremblay, Michel, 1942–
[Passé antérieur. English]
    Past perfect / Michel Tremblay ; translated by Linda Gaboriau.

    A play.
    Traduction de: Le passé antérieur.
    ISBN 0-88922-493-5

    I. Gaboriau, Linda  II. Title. III. Title: Passé antérieur. English.

PS8539.R47P3713 2004        C842'.54        C2003-907298-3

ISBN-13: 978-0-88922-493-3

*for André Brassard;*
*thirty-eight years of friendship,*
*twenty-two premieres,*
*a lifetime!*

*Le Passé antérieur* was first presented on February 19, 2003, at the Théâtre Jean-Duceppe in a production directed by André Brassard.

VICTOIRE . . . . . . . . . . . Rita Lafontaine
ALBERTINE . . . . . . . Violette Chauveau
ÉDOUARD. . . . . . . . . . . Vincent Giroux
MADELEINE . . . . . . . . . . . Isabel Richer
ALEX . . . . . . . . . . . . . Sylvain Bélanger
Set: Claude Goyette
Costumes: François Barbeau
Lighting: Éric Champoux
Music: Catherine Gadouas
Assistant Director: Carol Gagné

The first English-language production of *Past Perfect* was produced by Centaur Theatre Company, Montreal, Québec. Its premiere presentation took place on January 29, 2004 at Centaur Theatre under the artistic direction of Gordon McCall, with the following cast:

VICTOIRE . . . . . . . . . . . Donna Belleville
ALBERTINE . . . . . . . . . . Catherine Allard
ÉDOUARD . . . . . . . . . Paul Thomas Manz
MADELEINE . . . . . . . . . . . Manon St-Jules
ALEX . . . . . . . . . . . . . . . . . . . Sasha Roiz
Directed by Jackie Maxwell
Set and Costume Design by Patrick Clark
Lighting Design by Spike Lyne
Assistant Director: Mindy Parfitt
Stage Manager: Merissa Tordjman
Apprentice Stage Manager: David LeBlanc

# CHARACTERS

VICTOIRE (in her fifties)
ALBERTINE (20)
ÉDOUARD (19)
MADELEINE (18)
ALEX (23)

*Montreal, 1930.*

*The living room of a basement apartment in Old Montreal, Fortifications Alley. ALBERTINE, all dressed up to go out, is reading a glossy magazine that clashes with the humble surroundings. Enter VICTOIRE who has gone to fetch a pail of coal.*

VICTOIRE:
> What are you doing all dressed up in your Sunday best like that?

ALBERTINE:
> What's the matter? Can't I put on some decent clothes when I feel like it?

VICTOIRE:
> Not on Thursday! You'd think it was Easter Sunday before high mass ... Not that you and high mass ... I've never seen you dressed up like that on a Thursday night, except ... Oh, right ... It's Alex's night—

ALBERTINE:
> (*to change the subject*) Look at you, wearing your hat, just to go fetch some coal!

VICTOIRE:
> You never know who you might meet, young lady!

ALBERTINE:
> In the cellar! You put on your stupid little black straw hat just to get some coal at the back of the cellar!

VICTOIRE:

   Occasionally I meet somebody—

ALBERTINE:

   Somebody! What kind of somebody! The people
   who rent apartments here are poorer than we are!
   Half the time they can't even pay their rent and
   you're the first one to know that!

VICTOIRE:

   Just because you're a janitor in the poor end of town
   doesn't mean you've got no dignity!

ALBERTINE:

   You're not the janitor, Pa is. And no straw hat is
   going to win back your dignity ... not even a black
   one!

VICTOIRE:

   Your father would rather crawl around on all fours
   dead drunk than get down on all fours to wash the
   stairs, so somebody's got to do his job for him!

ALBERTINE:

   Here we go, you have to put him down! That's all
   you ever do!

VICTOIRE:

   He doesn't need anyone to put him down, Bertine,
   he does fine on his own. When you found him at the
   foot of the stairs last week, did he need anyone to
   put him down?

ALBERTINE:

   He just slipped!

VICTOIRE:

He slipped in his own—Aw, there's no point talking about him! And if I put him down, let's just say you idealize him something awful!

ALBERTINE:

I don't idealize him!

VICTOIRE:

You look at him and you see what you want to see, period!

ALBERTINE:

So do you! It's the same thing!

VICTOIRE:

That's not true, believe me. If you only knew how much I'd like to see something different from what I see.

ALBERTINE:

Oh, yeah ... like what?

VICTOIRE:

I don't know ... what he showed me when he was courting me!

ALBERTINE:

You've been married for twenty years!

VICTOIRE:

That's what I mean. The man I married disappeared twenty years ago ... the man I married lasted for six months, and I've been putting up with this one for twenty years. Day and night! Charm before harm ... that's marriage in a nutshell. I'm telling you, it wasn't long before the little love notes and the sweet kisses disappeared ... Oh, there's been other notes, but asking me to forgive him ... and his kisses tasted of beer ... Before they probably tasted of toothpaste and mouthwash and I didn't realize it ... The only man I'd ever kissed before never tasted of beer. Never! He tasted of hard liquor during the holidays, but the rest of the year he tasted of the countryside.

ALBERTINE:
And we never knew who he was.

VICTOIRE:
And you never will either.

ALBERTINE:
Gabriel says he knows who it was.

VICTOIRE:
Gabriel doesn't know any more than you kids do.

ALBERTINE:
Gabriel says that he was his real father.

VICTOIRE:
Gabriel can think what he wants.

ALBERTINE:
Is my big brother right? Is that it? Is your famous mystery lover his father? Do we know him? Is he still alive?

VICTOIRE:
You've been asking the same questions for ten years, you don't think I'm going to answer tonight, do you?

ALBERTINE:
I've been asking them since the day I realized Gabriel was ten years old when you married our

father … Me and Édouard and Madeleine are the
right age, but Gabriel—

VICTOIRE:

Why are you dredging that up again tonight? What's
the point?

ALBERTINE:

You're the one who mentioned the mysterious beau
first.

VICTOIRE:

Well, excuse me and forget I ever mentioned it. I
better get this pail of coal to the kitchen …

*She picks up the pail she'd set down on the floor.*

VICTOIRE:

Don't have to worry 'bout you helping me …

ALBERTINE:

Dressed like this? Fat chance!

VICTOIRE:

You've always got some reason. Not necessarily a
good one, but some reason. What did you all
promise me, you and your brother and your sister,
when your father accepted this job and we all knew
very well that he'd never do it because it was
beneath him, beneath what he thinks of himself,
who he thinks he is? Don't you remember?

ALBERTINE:

When I get home from the restaurant, I don't feel
like getting down on my hands and knees to scrub
the stairs or dragging out the vinegar to wash the
windows in the front hall. That shouldn't be so hard
to understand! I'm not a good person, Ma, you

know that. I don't like helping people. I'm not a
good person. You decided that years ago, and there's
nothing I can do now to change your mind. I
inherited Pa's poetic side—

VICTOIRE:

You, a poet! Don't make me laugh!

ALBERTINE:

What d'you mean?

VICTOIRE:

I can't imagine you reciting poems to the full moon,
or spending your evenings reading the complete
works of Victor Hugo, in twelve volumes. You want
to be like your father, Bertine, we all know that, you
want it too much and you'll never succeed. You
worship him, you'd love to be like him, a useless day-
dreamer, but you're not at all alike … unless, maybe
… yes … there's one thing … you're lazy like him, if
there's any resemblance, that's it!

ALBERTINE:

I beg your pardon, I'm not lazy. I break my neck ten
hours a day serving spaghetti 'n' meatballs to a
bunch of beggars who leave me a nickel tip if I'm
lucky, that's not what I call being lazy!

VICTOIRE:

Because they pay you to do it!

ALBERTINE:

I should hope so!

VICTOIRE:

But for everything else, you're lazy like him, and
sneaky like him too. When you don't feel like doing

something you've been asked to do, you start buttering up your brother and sister, and the first thing we know, one of them is doing your job! I don't know how you do it, but you always manage. Just like your father!

ALBERTINE:

(*a little grin*) That's not laziness ...

> Silence. VICTOIRE *stares at* ALBERTINE.

ALBERTINE:

You see, I'm more like him than you think.

VICTOIRE:

I don't know what to do with you.

ALBERTINE:

You've been telling me that ten times a day, since the day I was born.

> VICTOIRE *takes off her hat.*

ALBERTINE:

When I get home from work and I see you down on all fours washing the floor in the hall wearing your silly little straw hat, believe me, I don't find you so dignified ...

VICTOIRE:

I'm not asking you to, either. I could do it in a ball gown and it wouldn't change a thing. I'm not surprised that you don't understand the little straw hat, Bertine ... And I don't ask you to do anything anymore, because you judged me a long time ago and I'm afraid I've been condemned. In the meantime, go change your clothes. You look ridiculous dressed up like that on a Thursday night, when no one's coming to see you.

ALBERTINE:
You just said you don't ask me to do anything anymore …

VICTOIRE:
*I'm not asking you, Bertine, I'm ordering you!*

ALBERTINE:
If you can wash your floors wearing your straw hat, you can put up with me wearing decent clothes on a Thursday night.

VICTOIRE:
(*more quietly*) It's not the dress that bothers me, you know darn well. It's why you're wearing it on a Thursday night.

ALBERTINE:
That's my business.

VICTOIRE:
It'll be mine if you have another nervous breakdown.

ALBERTINE:
I didn't ask you for anything when I had my breakdown.

VICTOIRE:
You didn't see yourself lying in bed for two months, crying your eyes out, snivelling and cursing everyone … Acting like no one in the world deserved more pity than you!

ALBERTINE:

>I didn't want people to pity me.

VICTOIRE:

>Oh, yeah? You bawled louder every time anyone
>walked by your room! You did everything to attract
>attention. Like a twelve-year-old kid!

>*ALBERTINE stands up and struts by her mother.*

ALBERTINE:

>Look at me now ... Do I look like a twelve-year-old
>kid?

VICTOIRE:

>Maybe not, but you do look desperate for attention!
>And we all know whose attention and we know what
>the result will be. Nobody will pity you if you get
>hurt a second time. Nobody!

>*She exits carrying her pail of coal. ALBERTINE lights
>up a cigarette and tries to lose herself in her magazine.
>After a few seconds, she throws it on the floor.*

ALBERTINE:

>All I wanted ...

>*She picks up the magazine, smoothes the cover, puts it
>on the end table beside the sofa. She smokes her
>cigarette.*

ALBERTINE:

>All I wanted was ... I don't know ... a bit of ...
>something that felt like happiness, but I never
>would've called it happiness because I would've been
>too scared to lose it! Something ... I don't know how
>to say it ... something gentle ... I've never known
>anything gentle, except for my brother Édouard and

he's too gentle … Something I could've … drowned in? Is that the right word? Drowned? I guess so. It must be possible to drown in happiness. We're drowning in unhappiness around here! Well, maybe not everyone … This family's always been split down the middle … There's Pa and Ma and me … Pa loves us both, I think, in his own way … Ma hates both Pa and me … at least she resents us both … while me, I adore Pa and I can't stand Ma … but I can't say I hate her either … Hate takes too much energy … And there's the three other kids … Gabriel, the perfect son who married a perfect woman and has perfect kids, Madeleine, the dull one but not so dull, we realize that now, the damn hypocrite, and Édouard, who's gentle all right, a real softie. (*She takes a puff on her cigarette*) Something soft … gentle … and peaceful. Just a bit. Not too much. Just a tiny bit! Two peaceful people, alone together … two people who love each other. God, how stupid can you get! *How stupid can you get! And naïve!* Using a word like love after everything that's happened. How could I dream of that? Me, the kid who was born a month before my parents got married and who tries to be like my father because I want him to be my real father so bad, him, not some stranger or some hick from the country! Gabriel had another father too, he was born ten years before me, somewhere in the backwoods of the Laurentians … But it's different for him, of course, he's the oldest and he's a guy. Ma decided that he would succeed, and everything he does is perfect! It's easy to be perfect when everyone believes in you! (*Another puff on the cigarette.*) No big deal like in the movies … just something small … made to measure for me … Not too big for me to understand, for me to handle … (*Tears in her eyes.*) And to think I'd already found it!

*Enter VICTOIRE still holding her straw hat.*

VICTOIRE:

It shouldn't be that hard to understand … (*Pause.*) This hat, Bertine … When I'm down on my hands and knees washing the stairs and someone comes up or down … this hat tells them I'm not just the janitor's wife who's doing her husband's job because he's too lazy to do it himself, it tells them I'm a woman who still has her dignity and her pride, even if she's down on her hands and knees in front of them in a dirty staircase that stinks to high heaven! They can't see my grey hair all damp with sweat and my face all red with the effort, no, all they can see is black straw rocking back and forth, a little round hat they recognize because they've seen it a thousand times, and it demands their respect. You hear me, young lady? Their respect!

ALBERTINE:

C'mon! They laugh at you behind your back.

VICTOIRE:

I know everyone in the building calls me the little engine, but that's not because I wear a straw hat when I work, and it's not to laugh behind my back. It's because I'm efficient and I get things done fast! When they need something, they don't have to wait for days, I show up with my hammer and if I can, I fix it, right away! Yes, wearing my straw hat! And if I get too hot and too red in the face, I pull down my veil! And you know what, Bertine, if I could, I'd wash the floor wearing my kid gloves! They understand,

they call me Ma'am, clear as day, and they're happy
to see me ...

ALBERTINE:

Except at the end of the month ...

VICTOIRE:

We're in the middle of the Depression, Bertine,
people are dying of hunger left, right and centre,
open your eyes! You're lucky to work in a restaurant
... maybe there aren't as many customers as before,
but still. The American Spaghetti House will never
close because some people will always be able to
afford to go out for spaghetti, even if the world's
falling apart all around them. But this building is
full of people who've lost their jobs and who can't
feed themselves or pay their rent! And I'm sad to
have to go collect the ten dollars in rent that they're
sad to tell me they don't have. Don't tell me you've
forgotten we came to live here precisely because
your father lost his job as a translator! He wasn't
good at it, and he was badly paid, but at least it put
food on the table. All he managed to find six
months later was this job as a janitor at the end of
Fortifications Alley, and he took it because the
apartment came with it! He never intended to work
as a janitor. All he wanted was to live rent-free, and
to go on drinking his rubbing alcohol because beer
is too expensive!

ALBERTINE:

How can you say that!

VICTOIRE:

He's drinking himself to death, Bertine! He's killing
himself slowly but surely! You just don't want to

22

admit it, fine, that's not what we were talking about anyway! We were talking about my straw hat! Look, it's all creased and crushed, there are holes and the veil is torn ... But seen from above, in full motion, it still creates an illusion! And as long as it's wearable, I'm going to wear it, and you have nothing to say about it. If you're ashamed when you meet me in the staircase, pretend you don't see me! And just consider yourself lucky that I don't demand, that I don't *demand*, Bertine—because I'd have a right to— consider yourself lucky that I don't demand that you wash the damn stairs once in a while too!

ALBERTINE:

I'd like to see you try ...

VICTOIRE:

I'd like to see you refuse ...

ALBERTINE:

I already give you almost everything I earn! I hardly keep two miserable dollars a week for myself!

VICTOIRE:

Do you know how much it costs to feed five people in the middle of the Depression? Do you? Especially when there are only two little sources of income! You and your sister Madeleine feed us because your father and your brother don't work, and I'm really grateful because, if it weren't for that, there'd be no food on the table. But don't try to tell me you think it's fair for me to do a man's job just so we don't have to pay rent when the end of the month rolls 'round!

ALBERTINE:

    I never said I thought it was fair, I just said I wouldn't do it.

VICTOIRE:

    You'd have to do it if I insisted!

ALBERTINE:

    Go ahead, try!

VICTOIRE:

    You really don't understand, do you?

*She goes to sit on the sofa beside ALBERTINE.*

VICTOIRE:

    (*quietly*) I do everything I can to spare you and your sister, even if you both swore you'd help, because I know you're tired when you get home from work at night … I do it myself, so you don't have to do it … We are the janitors in this place and the janitor's job has to be done!

ALBERTINE:

    What about your fat son, eh? Why don't you *demand* that Édouard do it? The selfish blimp! Let him get down on all fours in the stairs once in a while, it'd do him good. No wonder he's so fat! He eats for twelve and he spends his days pretending to look for a job!

VICTOIRE:

    He is looking for a job!

ALBERTINE:

    He's not looking for a job, Ma, and he has no intention of finding one!

VICTOIRE:

> You can forgive your father for it, but not him?
> Anyway, Édouard is a special case.

ALBERTINE:

> Sure, there you go. Believe me, if I idealize Pa, you
> idealize Édouard something awful.

VICTOIRE:

> I don't idealize him ... I see exactly how he is.

ALBERTINE:

> So why do you always find excuses for him?

VICTOIRE:

> Because he's not made like the rest of us, Bertine.

ALBERTINE:

> What's that supposed to mean, he's not made like
> the rest of us?

VICTOIRE:

> Édouard isn't strong like the rest of us ...

ALBERTINE:

> Are you kidding? He's strong as a horse. I should
> know, we used to fight all the time when we were
> kids ... He's strong when it suits him, and he's weak
> when it can pay off. Open your eyes!

VICTOIRE:

> I mean inside. He's not made like the rest of us
> inside ... You and me, and Madeleine, and Gabriel,
> too ... we can ... I don't know ... we can take a lot,
> put up with a lot, you in the restaurant, Madeleine
> in the factory, Gabriel at the printer's, me with my
> straw hat ... but not him. Until he finds exactly what
> he should do in life, he'll go on being like that ...

25

I'm sure that when he finally finds the right job, it'll be for life … In the meantime, he's trying to find himself—

ALBERTINE:
And he does everything to make sure he doesn't! Poor baby … I feel so sorry for him! Spending his days hanging out downtown clowning around with his friends who are lazy loafers like him! You know what he says he wants to do in life, while you kill yourself washing stairs on your hands and knees with your hat on your head to preserve your dignity? He wants to be an actor in Hollywood! In the talkies! So he's not about to find a job for life tomorrow, right? You haven't finished feeding him! He's nineteen years old, dresses like a prince, he's got spending money and we all know where he gets it and he's not complaining! No wonder! I'd do the same thing in his place! Room and board and clothes for free!

VICTOIRE:
You're right, you look at him the way I look at your father … and I look at him the way you look at your father …

ALBERTINE:
And who do you think is right?

   *Silence.*

VICTOIRE:
If they're both lazy loafers, I'm doing all this for nothing because I've placed my hopes in my son. If they're both saints, being a saint is a snap, you just do nothing and let other people wait on you hand and foot … I should take a leaf out of their book!

*They laugh.*

ALBERTINE:
Sometimes you have a way of looking at things—

VICTOIRE:
I'm not as crazy as you think, you know.

ALBERTINE:
I never thought you were crazy. You're a real pain,
but you're not crazy.

VICTOIRE:
I guess that makes two of us, right ...

ALBERTINE:
I'd be less of a pain if more people listened to me
around here.

VICTOIRE:
Me too. But we're wasting our time talking about
these things, maybe we'll never settle them ...

ALBERTINE:
You think so?

VICTOIRE:
If you lock two stubborn mules up in the same box,
they'll drive each other so crazy, you'll end up taking
them both to the loony bin.

ALBERTINE:
So is that what's going to happen to us? Will we
drive each other crazy?

VICTOIRE:
I've already locked myself up in a box, Bertine. You
still have a chance to get away.

ALBERTINE:

 I had my chance. I lost it. It's all over.

VICTOIRE:

 That's nonsense. See how you are? You're only
 twenty, you've got your whole life ahead of you. One
 little heartbreak can't destroy that. One heartbreak
 isn't the end of the world, for heaven's sake!

ALBERTINE:

 One little heartbreak! *One little heartbreak!* I almost
 died of it, Ma!

VICTOIRE:

 Nonsense! Stop exaggerating! You didn't almost die
 of it at all!

ALBERTINE:

 I'm not twenty, Ma, I'm eighty. I could be your
 mother!

VICTOIRE:

 Don't you think I had my share of troubles when I
 was younger? But I never would've said something
 like that! I bawled, beat my fists on the floor and
 when it was over, I stood up and got on with my life!

ALBERTINE:

 That's because you never had a real heartbreak. You
 never recover from the kind of heartbreak I had,
 never!

VICTOIRE:

 If it's a contest you're looking for, let me say one
 thing, young lady … Your heartbreak a few months
 ago was ridiculous compared to the one I lived
 through, the one I've never told you about and

never will, even though you've been quizzing me for years!

ALBERTINE:
Who's looking for a contest now?

VICTOIRE:
I'm just telling you that so you stop seeing yourself as a heroine in some novel, Bertine.

ALBERTINE:
I don't see myself as a heroine in a novel ...

VICTOIRE:
What you went through, Bertine, is very sad, and we all felt bad for you, but it's over now, a thing of the past and it's not the end of the world!

ALBERTINE:
My beau left me for my sister who's two years younger than me and you say that's not the end of the world?

VICTOIRE:
No, it isn't. It's sad, but it's not the end of the world. First of all, he wasn't really your beau—

ALBERTINE:
What do you mean, not really my beau! He certainly was!

VICTOIRE:
You only went out a couple of times.

ALBERTINE:
That's not true!

VICTOIRE:
Maybe a bit more.

ALBERTINE:

We went out together for almost a year, Ma!

VICTOIRE:

Did you? Really? Well, it wasn't that serious. At least it wasn't serious on his side, that was clear! But you got all carried away, you decided you were going to marry him, you pounced on him like a cat on a mouse, he was scared, the poor guy, no wonder!

ALBERTINE:

Is that how you see it?

VICTOIRE:

That's how it was, Bertine!

ALBERTINE:

That's not true!

VICTOIRE:

Yes, it is true! It's as clear as the nose on your face. All that guy wants is to have a good time with girls. He's a weathercock. He just started working with his father who's a travelling salesman, doesn't that say it all? You know the reputation travelling salesmen have! He's probably started to have a girl in every town, seducing all the housewives he wants to sell his products to … He's a charmer, a real charmer. Did you see his smile? Did you? Don't try to tell me that's the smile of a sincere man! It's the smile of a con-man, period!

ALBERTINE:

Well maybe he's different from other travelling salesmen. Maybe his smile is sincere and you don't want to see it!

VICTOIRE:

> You just have to take a good look at him to see what
> kind he is. Wake up!

ALBERTINE:

> He's so handsome!

VICTOIRE:

> Yes, and he thought you were beautiful, he liked you
> and he asked you to go out with him and you
> misread his intentions.

ALBERTINE:

> That's crazy!

VICTOIRE:

> Instead of having a good time with him, the way he
> wanted to have a good time with you, you took
> everything too seriously and he took off. That's all
> there is to it.

ALBERTINE:

> With my own sister! You think she doesn't take him
> seriously?

VICTOIRE:

> Of course she does. She's making the same mistake
> as you, and I should have a talk with her, too!

ALBERTINE:

> What she did simply isn't done.

VICTOIRE:

> She didn't have to do anything, Bertine. You became
> so demanding with Alex he couldn't help looking
> elsewhere because you scared him ... and right there
> beside you was your little sister ... I better warn her
> too. Then there'll be another crisis in the house,

we'll spend another two months with a nervous breakdown in the back bedroom ... but I'd rather go through that than see her married to that character!

ALBERTINE:

It's her turn ... But I'm telling you I won't have her marrying him!

VICTOIRE:

(*after a brief silence*) What you're planning to do just isn't right, I hope you realize that.

ALBERTINE:

I'm not planning to do anything.

VICTOIRE:

Bertine, you're as subtle as a cat in heat.

ALBERTINE:

I'm no cat in heat. I wasn't thinking of anything like that!

VICTOIRE:

Then go change your clothes and make sure you don't run into Alex when he gets here—

ALBERTINE:

Oh, it's true, it's Thursday night, Alex will be coming—

VICTOIRE:

Bertine! Don't make me lose my temper! At least don't take me for a fool! It's obvious that's why you put that dress on, and I repeat, it's not right ... And you run the risk of being humiliated again. Think of that.

ALBERTINE:

I'd like to see him try.

VICTOIRE:

He's coming to see your sister, Bertine, it's finished, and there's no starting over.

ALBERTINE:

Starting over can happen, if you try hard enough ...

VICTOIRE:

You see how you are! Stubborn as a mule!

ALBERTINE:

I'm not the only one, you said so yourself ...

VICTOIRE:

Stay away from him, take my advice ... there are other guys ... guys who are nicer ... and more sincere, especially. Some day you'll meet one who'll make you happy, you're only twenty years old!

ALBERTINE:

He's the one I want.

VICTOIRE:

But he doesn't want you!

ALBERTINE:

I'll make sure that changes ...

VICTOIRE:

You wouldn't do that to your own sister!

ALBERTINE:

She did it to me!

VICTOIRE:

How many times do I have to tell you that's not true!
It was your own fault—

ALBERTINE:

Of course, it's always my own fault—

VICTOIRE:

That's not what I meant. God, talking to you is
impossible.

ALBERTINE:

That's right. Forget the talking and let me live my
life as I please.

VICTOIRE:

But no good can come of this! Let them be, Bertine,
forgive him, and forgive her, too, if you really think
it was her fault—

ALBERTINE:

Never!

VICTOIRE:

That's not love, Bertine! That's stubbornness! And
pride!

ALBERTINE:

Well, that's how it is, I've got my pride too! You wear
your straw hat to wash the floors, and I wear a new
dress to greet my sister's beau. So there!

VICTOIRE:

I guess you enjoy it.

ALBERTINE:

Enjoy what?

VICTOIRE:

    Danger. Playing with fire. Seeing how far you can go before everything blows up in your face!

ALBERTINE:

    Not true. You've got it all wrong ... I just want to take back what's rightfully mine.

VICTOIRE:

    You can't be serious.

ALBERTINE:

    I am.

VICTOIRE:

    There's no sense talking about it then ... When you've made up your mind like that, there's nothing anybody can say or do ...

    *Commotion can be heard in the hallway.*

ALBERTINE:

    Exactly.

VICTOIRE:

    We're impotent, we just have to shut up and grin and bear it ... There's Édouard and Madeleine. Watch what you do, Bertine ... Because in the long run, you're the one who'll suffer most.

    *MADELEINE and ÉDOUARD enter laughing.*

ÉDOUARD:

    You're kidding me. That's not true.

MADELEINE:

    It is true! Besides he told me himself. He was red as a beet—

*She notices ALBERTINE.*

MADELEINE:

What are you doing wearing that dress?

ÉDOUARD:

Yeah, it's not even yours.

VICTOIRE:

That dress isn't yours?

MADELEINE:

Ma, tell her to take it off immediately, I bought it to
wear on my date next Saturday night—

ALBERTINE:

I just borrowed it, for god's sake … And since when
do you have enough money to buy yourself a dress?
Everyone's starving to death! We're in the middle of
a Depression! We'll share it, okay? I'll pay for half of
your damn dress.

MADELEINE: ·

It was on sale, and it's none of your business anyway!
I can do what I want with the money I save.

ÉDOUARD:

If you didn't go to the movies so often, Bertine, you
could buy yourself some new dresses.

ALBERTINE:

Look who's talking! If you didn't stuff your face so
much, you could buy yourself some new dresses, too.

ÉDOUARD:

Very funny! What's that supposed to mean?

ALBERTINE:

Aw, forget it … (*to MADELEINE*) I just wanted to try it on, Madeleine.

VICTOIRE:

I don't want to listen to this. (*to MADELEINE*) When you two have stopped squabbling, I want to talk to you … (*to ALBERTINE*) If you've got an ounce of decency, Bertine, go take that dress off immediately! In the meantime, I'm going to peel the potatoes. We've got to eat, right?

*She exits.*

MADELEINE:

You heard what Ma just said …

ALBERTINE:

Okay, I'll take it off, in a while—

MADELEINE:

Not in a while, now! Immediately! She said immediately!

ALBERTINE:

Hey, the house isn't on fire! Were you going to wear it tonight? Wasn't it for Saturday night?

MADELEINE:

Oh, my god! I just remembered, Alex is coming tonight!

ÉDOUARD:

Oops!

MADELEINE:

Wait a minute …

ALBERTINE:

> Relax, Madeleine, I couldn't care less about that guy
> …

ÉDOUARD:

> Of course not—

ALBERTINE:

> Shut your trap! Do I stick my nose in your business?
> You're always snooping around everywhere! Go help
> Ma peel the potatoes, like a good girl!

ÉDOUARD:

> I told you I don't find your stupid jokes funny.

ALBERTINE:

> And I told you that I don't find your dumb puss
> funny! Your chubby little face that always shows up
> whenever there's any trouble! Go get into some
> trouble of you own, instead of feeding off other
> people's problems!

ÉDOUARD:

> Well, well! Look at that. Suddenly it's the sermon on
> the mount! Are you going to start telling us how to
> live our lives again? I thought that was all over. We
> had peace and quiet for a while. During your
> nervous breakdown, you left us alone. Don't tell me
> you're going to start in again!

ALBERTINE:

> Go to hell!

ÉDOUARD:

> Your life is such a great success!

ALBERTINE:

> At least I earn my own living!

ÉDOUARD:

When I start to earn mine, I'm going to make a
fortune and you'll be green with envy.

ALBERTINE:

Right, in Hollywood, maybe! You're nineteen years
old and you're still dreaming like a kid. Hollywood!
First you better lose a hundred pounds and learn to
speak English!

ÉDOUARD:

I get along in English just fine. And if I lost twenty
pounds, I'd be perfectly presentable! Besides,
Hollywood was just a joke.

ALBERTINE:

I should hope so! Because they can get along
without you!

ÉDOUARD:

Anyway, seeing you dressed up like Madeleine, we all
know who you can't get along without!

> *He bursts out laughing. She throws her ashtray at
> him. He runs off laughing.*

ÉDOUARD:

I'd love to hear this conversation!

ALBERTINE:

I believe it ... (*to MADELEINE, after a rather long
embarrassed pause*) You haven't said a thing. The cat
got your tongue?

MADELEINE:

No, I just don't know what to say ... I'm so shocked I
can't find the words—

ALBERTINE:

Shocked? You've got no reason to be shocked!

MADELEINE:

I feel like going to my room to cry my eyes out ... or like strangling you.

ALBERTINE:

My God! All that for a little dress you bought on sale!

MADELEINE:

That's what's so incredible about you, Bertine, you take us all for idiots!

ALBERTINE:

I don't take you all for idiots if you don't act like idiots ...

MADELEINE:

C'mon ... be honest for once ... Put your cards on the table.

ALBERTINE:

What's that supposed to mean? That I'm cheating?

MADELEINE:

Cheating? You spend your life cheating! The word was invented for you! You manipulate everyone in this household, you set us up against each other, you're the one who's always right, and we all have to do what you want, everything you want, day in and day out! You say one thing to one person, and something else to the next. Do you think we don't know that! Do you think we don't talk to each other? Life goes on when you're not around, you know!

You're the worst liar I know, Bertine, and like all
liars, you think you're too smart to get caught!

ALBERTINE:

My God, when you let go, you let go!

MADELEINE:

And you don't listen when people talk to you! It
goes in one ear and out the other. No matter what
we say, no matter how hard we try to explain things,
nothing sinks in. It's like you decide to pull the plug.
No matter how hard we tug on the little chain,
nothing lights up!

ALBERTINE:

Go ahead, tell me I'm not smart, to top it all off!

MADELEINE:

You see, even when you are listening, you manage to
twist things around. I'm not saying you're not smart,
Bertine, I'm saying that whatever we tell you slides
off you like water off a duck's back! No one can ever
win an argument with you, because you fight no
holds barred. You hit where it hurts most, even if it's
completely off the subject.

ALBERTINE:

Right, that's it, a real monster.

MADELEINE:

Right, that's it, a real monster.

ALBERTINE:

Forget about me then. Leave the monster alone in
its corner like a rat.

MADELEINE:

You see what I mean. That's typical! You're twisting the conversation around and the next thing we know, you're the one we should feel sorry for, and we're the ones who are heartless! And how do you expect me to leave you alone in a corner like a rat? We sleep in the same room! We've never had our own rooms because our apartments have always been too small. We spent our whole childhood and our adolescence putting up with each other in the same little bedroom because we had no choice, but the months you spent in bed, not so long ago, complaining and bawling all day and all night, how do you think that was for me? I didn't complain because I knew how sad you were, I knew you were really suffering, but believe me, it was pretty darn depressing in that bedroom! I know what you're going to say, it wasn't the same for me, and it's true it was worse for you, but do you know how often I came to sleep here in the living room because I was sick of listening to you sniffle and blow your nose? I didn't have a room anymore. I'm not blaming you, I know how hard it was for you, but did you ever think about me even once, Bertine? Did you ever think, maybe I should make an effort, poor Madeleine has to put up with me? Never! It was a one-way street! I bothered you and you let me know it by sighing impatiently every time I set foot in the room.

ALBERTINE:

I hope you're not trying to convince me we should feel sorry for you. Not with … Aw, forget it, there's no point talking about it.

MADELEINE:

On the contrary! Go ahead, say it! C'mon, show us your hand. That's what I'm waiting for, Bertine. Look me in the eye and tell me, instead of whining to Ma the way I bet you already did, blaming everything on everyone else.

*ALBERTINE goes to pick up the ashtray, places it on the end table and lights up a cigarette.*

ALBERTINE:

(*quietly*) Let me have him, Madeleine.

MADELEINE:

Tell me you didn't say that. Bertine, do you realize how many times you've said that to me in your life? "Let me have it, Madeleine." Whenever we got presents when we were kids ... they were never big presents because we were never rich, but we were happy to get them anyway. The minute we opened the box or tore off the paper, Gabriel, Édouard or me, you wanted whatever was inside.

*ALBERTINE shrugs her shoulders.*

MADELEINE:

It's true! Gabriel would try to explain that it wasn't yours, that it wasn't your birthday or that you had your own Christmas present, but you refused to listen. You'd say you just wanted to see it up close or touch it. But we knew if we let you hold it, we'd never see it again, or you'd pretend it was yours and you wouldn't want to give it back ... Even though you were older than Édouard and me! And you got just as many presents as us! You tried everything, tantrums and tears, calling us selfish because we never wanted to share with you, and if that didn't

43

work, you'd look all pathetic and whine: "Let me have it." As if it was the most important thing in the world for you, but you were really doing it just to take it away from us! We wouldn't have minded sharing our presents with you, Bertine, lending them for you to play with, but not the minute we took them out of the wrapping! Not before we even had time to see what it was and how it worked! But you couldn't help it, you couldn't wait. You had to have everything for yourself. Tin soldiers you didn't even care about, a pair of pants that wouldn't fit you, oranges you always hated! And now you dare say the same thing about my beau!

ALBERTINE:
Who, according to Ma, is no great shakes, but that's a whole other story ...

MADELEINE:
You see, now you're ready to make a joke of it all ... Even though I know very well it's no joke, you're serious and you think that all you have to do is ask and I'll give you my beau.

ALBERTINE:
He was mine before he was yours.

MADELEINE:
He was yours before he was mine. You lost him, and I found him, Bertine! That's how it is.

ALBERTINE:
Oh, you and your scheming! You must've been plotting for ages—

MADELEINE:

I've got my faults but I'm not a schemer and you
know it. I didn't even notice Alex when you were
going out with him. He was your beau, he was really
handsome, looked like he had a sense of humour,
he smelled nice, but I never would've thought …
Anyway, what's the point of rehashing all this, you're
making me waste my breath. I didn't have to run
after him, he's the one who came looking for me.

ALBERTINE:

And you never asked yourself why?

MADELEINE:

Why what?

ALBERTINE:

Why he came looking for you.

MADELEINE:

I don't get what you mean …

ALBERTINE:

Why he came looking for you instead of going to see
the woman down the street or some girl who lives
miles away from here …

MADELEINE:

Well, I don't know, because I was there all along,
he'd see me, he must've liked what he saw … How
do I know—

ALBERTINE:

Because you were my sister, Madeleine! Because you
were my sister and he knew that would kill me!

MADELEINE:

Wait a minute, what are you getting at?

ALBERTINE:

> He wasn't satisfied with casting me off like a pair of
> old boots, he decided to chase after *my sister*! To
> hurt me even more! He knew I'd see him when he
> came calling for you, that I'd hear him ring the bell,
> hear him talking loud, laughing, that I'd smell his
> after-shave that would linger in the house after the
> two of you left ... You silly girl, sometimes you're so
> naïve ... He's using you so he can go on pissing me
> off!

MADELEINE:

> Bertine! If Ma heard you talking like that in this
> house!

ALBERTINE:

> Forget Ma! Ma comes out with some good ones
> when it suits her. Now you're the one who's
> changing the subject.

MADELEINE:

> I'm changing the subject because you're talking
> nonsense.

ALBERTINE:

> Did you ever ask him? Eh? Did you ask him why he's
> going out with you rather than someone else?

MADELEINE:

> Of course I asked him. Sooner or later you ask that
> question—

ALBERTINE:

> And? And what did he say? Huh?

MADELEINE:

What he said is none of your business! You hear me, Bertine, none of your business! What goes on between him and me is none of your business. Just because you used to go out with him doesn't mean we have to report to you on his comings and goings and everything he says.

ALBERTINE:

Anyway, I'm sure he didn't tell you the truth.

MADELEINE:

Because you're the one who knows the truth.

ALBERTINE:

You bet! I just told you the truth ...

MADELEINE:

Yeah, right ... You always relate everything to you. The centre of the universe! The universe revolves around little old you. Everything, absolutely everything, is related to you! I suppose they brought on the Depression just so you'd earn less at the American Spaghetti House? It's impossible that Alex could simply love me. No! It must have something to do with the centre of the universe, my sister Albertine! Anyway, in case you're interested, he did tell me why he dumped you!

ALBERTINE:

I know why he dumped me.

MADELEINE:

Oh yeah, why?

ALBERTINE:

Because I was too intense. Too demanding.

MADELEINE:

That's one way of putting it. There are others.

ALBERTINE:

Oh really? Let's hear it.

MADELEINE:

Because you were unbearable, Bertine! It's as simple
as that. Because no man could put up with you! You
were jealous, possessive, you couldn't stand him
looking at another woman, even if she was standing
right in front of him in the street, he was supposed
to pay attention to you, only you, and he wasn't
supposed to notice anything or anyone else. When
he went to eat at the American Spaghetti House, he
should have put blinkers on to make sure he never
noticed the people sitting next to him! If you
could've controlled his brain, you would have!
Seventy-five per cent of your dates ended with you
making a scene, giving him hell, threatening him
because you were jealous or felt neglected the
minute his attention wasn't focussed on you. Do you
think he wanted to spend the rest of his life like
that, the prisoner of a hysterical woman who was
always carrying on trying to get his attention? He's a
travelling salesman, Bertine. What would you have
done when he was on the road? Would you have
followed him like a slave?

ALBERTINE:

That's what it means to be in love, Madeleine. You
surrender completely and you expect the other
person to do the same!

MADELEINE:

It's all very fine, to surrender completely, as long as you don't go crazy!

ALBERTINE:

Well, that's where you're wrong, Madeleine! That's where everyone's wrong! There's nothing more beautiful than being crazy in love. And if you don't realize that, if you've never known what that means, not even with him, then too bad for you! I know what it means, I knew what it meant with him, I was crazy about him, I let myself be crazy about him, and I'll never regret it! He was everything to me. Nothing, nothing else mattered in my life, Madeleine, it was complete, that was all I wanted, all I needed! All I needed. And it would have been all I needed till the end of my days! Maybe it's true that I was demanding, but I think love is meant to be demanding. When you get married, you're married for life! For life! That's huge! And with him, life would've been too short! Nothing, no stroke of bad luck or unhappiness could have defeated me! I would've been able to face everything with him! Do you love him like that? Do you? Do you love him that much?

MADELEINE:

In my own way, yes—

ALBERTINE:

Yeah, in your own way ... your lukewarm way ... You'll love him a little bit, for a little while ... Then, because you're only eighteen, you'll move on to the next one ... But I never, *never would have moved on to someone else.*

MADELEINE:

That's what you say because it still hurts—

ALBERTINE:

You just wait ... You'll see in five years when I turn twenty-five and still haven't married, people will start saying that I'll stay an old maid because I loved someone too much when I was young ...

MADELEINE:

You're stubborn enough to make it come true ...

ALBERTINE:

Whenever people talk about me, it always comes down to that, doesn't it? Stubborn as a mule. That's what Ma said to me a little while ago, now it's your turn ... You're not very original.

MADELEINE:

It's not a question of originality, Bertine. It's clear as day to anybody who's known you for five minutes! It's written on your forehead, in your pigheaded attitude: stubborn as a mule.

ALBERTINE:

Honestly! First the mule, now the pig! Maybe we'll go through the whole barnyard! How 'bout a silly goose?

*She lights up another cigarette.*

MADELEINE:

And you smoke too much, too.

ALBERTINE:

*Could you all stop criticizing me all the time!*

MADELEINE:
Maybe you could start behaving yourself too!

ALBERTINE:
What's that supposed to mean—behave yourself?
Behave like the rest of you? Behave like you? I don't
feel like dying of boredom!

MADELEINE:
Here we go …

ALBERTINE:
That's right, back to square one. Nothing's settled,
but we can at least try to get to the bottom of one
thing. Get Alex to talk, Madeleine, get him to tell
you why he became interested in you right after
dumping me.

MADELEINE:
I can't ask him about something that doesn't exist,
something that only exists in your head! He told me
that what he likes about me is that I'm calm and
gentle …

ALBERTINE:
Oh, really! And he told me that what he liked about
me was my passion and my energy! He should make
up his mind! Does he want to be bored or does he
want something to happen in his life?

MADELEINE:
Maybe he did appreciate your passion and your
energy, Bertine … I never claimed he didn't love
you …

ALBERTINE:
I'd like to see you try!

MADELEINE:

At first, I refused to go out with him ...

ALBERTINE:

Oh, really? That's a new one.

MADELEINE:

No, it's not new. You just didn't want to see it when it was happening.

ALBERTINE:

Right, because I wasn't listening. We all know I never listen to anyone.

MADELEINE:

I refused to go out with him because I was your sister, Bertine. I thought it just wasn't done. I wasn't about to have a visit from my sister's ex-beau while she was still crying her eyes out in our back bedroom! I have more of a conscience than you think, you see? But as time went by ... As time went by, I figured you'd get over it, that nobody could go on suffering like that ... And after a while, it got to me ... I didn't dislike him, he kept sending me flowers, boxes of chocolates, in the middle of the Depression ... You realize how much chocolates cost these days? And I ended up believing him when he said he realized that he'd made a mistake, and it was me he was in love with.

ALBERTINE:

What?! He told you that? He dared tell you that? You see! I told you! That's proof that I'm the one he's trying to get to. That he's using you to hurt me! Well, he's succeeded, he hurt me something awful. I should go out and buy a gun and shoot him dead!

MADELEINE:

I prefer it when you talk like that, Bertine! You should hate him, that's exactly what you should do!

ALBERTINE:

*But I love him too much to hate him!* He's still too much a part of my life, I can still hear his voice, his laugh, and I feel like his after-shave will cling to my fingers forever! Let me have him, Madeleine!

MADELEINE:

Stop saying that! Even if I wanted to let you have him, he doesn't want anything to do with you! It's his life, and he's got a right to do what he wants with it.

ALBERTINE:

Then let him dump you, too! What does he think he's doing in this house, if he doesn't want anything to do with me? Let him go find his women somewhere else and leave my family alone! And if he's cut out of the cloth of all travelling salesmen, if he's hell bent on being a bastard with a woman in every town he visits, then he shouldn't get married, he should stay a bachelor and leave us alone, for god's sake, he should leave us the hell alone!

MADELEINE:

(*very quietly*) Alex loves me, Bertine. Whether you like it or not. For once, something you refuse to accept will go on existing. And I wouldn't be surprised if he asked me to marry him soon ...

*ALBERTINE is stunned. She puts her hand on her heart.*

MADELEINE:

That's right ... You might have to live with that pain for the rest of your life if you're not willing to change. Because you're the one who has to change, Bertine. I'm sorry, but I refuse to sacrifice my happiness because it might hurt you ...

ALBERTINE:

Are you sure ... that he's going to ask you to marry him?

MADELEINE:

Yes. So your little scene with my new dress won't get you anywhere. Anyway, it's ridiculous to try to seduce him by dressing up like me.

ALBERTINE:

I wasn't trying to seduce him by dressing up like you ... I just didn't have a decent dress to wear ... and you've never worn this one, he wouldn't have known—

MADELEINE:

But you were trying to seduce him ...

*ALBERTINE doesn't answer.*

MADELEINE:

Don't do it, Bertine. You'll only feel worse. And don't go thinking I'm scared, I'm not at all scared ... You're not a threat to me ... Listen ... I've got to go wash up and change, we're going out for supper. Nothing fancy, something simple. He'll be coming any minute now. Don't stay here in the living room. Go to your room.

*ALBERTINE still doesn't answer.*

MADELEINE:

I'm going to send Édouard as a chaperone, just in case …

*She heads for the living room door.*

MADELEINE:

You don't want to be rejected again, Bertine. You can't win, you've already lost, period … Accept it once and for all …

*She exits. ALBERTINE goes over to the living room window, looks outside. She looks at her watch. ÉDOUARD appears and leans against the door frame.*

ÉDOUARD:

How many times have I seen you do that … is he on his way, is he almost here, what time is it anyway, feels like he's late …

ALBERTINE:

Go ahead, rub salt in the wound.

ÉDOUARD:

I wouldn't rub if you hadn't started first.

ALBERTINE:

My eye. There's nothing you like more in life than to get my goat.

ÉDOUARD:

I'd do it less, if I didn't get a rise out of you.

ALBERTINE:

I can't help it, I'm all nerves.

*ÉDOUARD smiles.*

ÉDOUARD:

You can say that again.

ALBERTINE:

And you always took advantage of it, you and
Gabriel.

ÉDOUARD:

(*quietly*) As far as that goes ... for us, it was just for
fun ... It's still just for fun, I hope you realize that, I
hope you don't think I try to get your goat to make
you feel bad and "add to your misery," as they say in
Ma's novels ... But you always took it seriously. To
the bitter end. Never reached the point where you'd
laugh and say to us: "Get off my back!" and take a
swat at us, like they do in other families where
brothers tease their sisters, like they do everywhere
and always have done ... And it didn't change after
Gabriel left home. You act like every joke I make
about you is high treason, Bertine ...

ALBERTINE:

So why don't you stop, if you don't get a kick out of
it anymore?

ÉDOUARD:

Who said I don't get a kick out of it? On the
contrary! Nothing's more fun than getting her
Majesty's goat!

ALBERTINE:

So, one way or another, I have to put up with your
stupid jokes.

ÉDOUARD:

'Fraid so.

ALBERTINE:

> All the more reason to get the hell out of here as soon as I can.

ÉDOUARD:

> That's new, now you want to get out of here …

ALBERTINE:

> Just because you didn't know doesn't mean it's new …

ÉDOUARD:

> Where would you go?

ALBERTINE:

> You'd be the last one to know, believe me!

> *ALBERTINE has gone back to sit on the sofa and lights up another cigarette. ÉDOUARD sighs.*

ALBERTINE:

> I know, I smoke too much and its stinks, but it calms my nerves …

> *ÉDOUARD goes to sit beside her.*

ÉDOUARD:

> Why don't you loosen up a bit, Bertine?

ALBERTINE:

> What?

ÉDOUARD:

> Loosen up a bit. You act like what you're going through was carved in stone two hundred years before Christ, and they should be teaching it to us in school!

ALBERTINE:

I don't get what you mean.

ÉDOUARD:

You get it alright. If you didn't take things so seriously all the time, if you took, I don't know, ten or fifteen per cent of it with a sense of humour, you'd be a lot happier!

ALBERTINE:

Humour! Do you see any humour in what's happened to me?! My beau dumps me so he can go out with my kid sister … and you find that humorous!

ÉDOUARD:

You see, your lack of sense of humour makes you change the course of events.

ALBERTINE:

Are you saying my sister isn't going out with my ex-beau?

ÉDOUARD:

He is, but he didn't dump you in order to go out with her! That part's not true! It was months before he asked her to go out with him.!

ALBERTINE:

It all comes down to the same thing!

ÉDOUARD:

It's not the same thing at all.

ALBERTINE:

Yes, it does come down to the same thing. The result is the same!

ÉDOUARD:

No, Bertine! It's less tragic! And that's what you can't accept! If he'd started going out with her while he was still going out with you, if they'd done it behind your back, both of them, and you caught them behind a door, or in the back of the closet, then that would be awful, then you'd have every reason to be as furious as you are … But that's not how it happened, and you know that! He had the decency, the decency, Bertine, to wait for months, hoping you'd feel better, before he asked Madeleine to go out with him …

ALBERTINE:

Decency! You call that decency?! Are you looking for a slap in the face?

ÉDOUARD:

If you loosened up a bit, if you could detach yourself a bit, get a bit of distance, you'd see that what happened isn't that awful, and maybe you could even laugh about it … There's lots of other guys, Bertine, Montreal's full of them! You're a pretty girl, you're young, you wouldn't have any trouble finding a guy who's better-looking, nicer, richer! Laugh at him a bit! If you can't laugh at yourself, at least laugh at him! I can't remember the last time I saw you laugh, I don't know if I ever saw you laugh!

ALBERTINE:

Only dopes like you laugh at everything.

ÉDOUARD:

Thanks!

ALBERTINE:

> You're welcome! I'd like to know how you'd react if
> your girlfriend left you for another guy. Mind you,
> no chance of that happening to you.

ÉDOUARD:

> What's that supposed to mean?

ALBERTINE:

> Forget it ... not only do I not laugh, not only do I
> have zero sense of humour, on top of that, there are
> subjects I avoid like the plague, just *in case* they'd
> make me laugh!

ÉDOUARD:

> I know what you're referring to, Bertine, and I'm
> sure it wouldn't make you laugh at all.

ALBERTINE:

> You're right. It wouldn't make me laugh. Not even
> that could make me laugh. And as far as loosening
> up goes ... Do you think I wouldn't like to? Do you
> think I don't wish I was different? Do you think I
> chose to be this way? That I wouldn't prefer to have
> something other than bad luck in my life?

ÉDOUARD:

> You attract bad luck ...

ALBERTINE:

> Sure, that's what Ma says! A magnet for bad luck, is
> that it?

ÉDOUARD:

> No, that's the point, you're not a magnet for bad
> luck ... Bad luck doesn't just strike out of nowhere,

by accident, because someone happens to be there when bad luck is passing by!

ALBERTINE:

Here we go again ... I'm the one who goes looking for it, is that it? Well, save your saliva, Ma's been telling me that since the day I was born ...

ÉDOUARD:

And did you ever stop to think she might be right?

ALBERTINE:

As far as you're concerned, Ma's always right! She's perfect, and she knows everything.

ÉDOUARD:

Don't change the subject, Bertine! Leave Ma out of this.

ALBERTINE:

I know what you want me to say, and I won't say it because I don't believe it! You hear me? You can laugh as much as you want, you can go through life grinning from ear to ear, but leave me alone! You've never gone through this kind of humiliation, you're too young, so you don't know what you're talking about!

ÉDOUARD:

Who says that I haven't been through another kind, maybe worse? And maybe I somehow managed to rise above it? Do you think life is easy for a guy who looks like me? Don't you all wonder why I'm always rushing around, why I can't stay still, why I talk so fast and so loud ... It's to escape, Bertine. I'm always trying to escape something or someone! I tell myself, if I keep moving, if I take up a lot of space, make a

lot of fuss, people will notice less how I look and
more what I can do! I push my talents because my
body isn't much to look at. I make light of
everything so people won't notice how heavy I am!
And have you ever thought about my love life, about
the kind of love life I can hope to have, or are you
too caught up in your personal tragedies to think
about your kid brother's problems?

ALBERTINE:

I don't feel like talking about that either. Not
because they're your problems, but because I'm not
interested. Live the life you want, hang out with
whoever you want, but don't bring it home here!
When you walk out the door, I don't know where
you go, and I don't want to know. I don't want to
know who you hang out with, I don't want to know
what you do, and if you go through humiliation
worse than mine and manage to rise above it, good
for you, but keep it to yourself, please!

ÉDOUARD:

Is that it? End of conversation? We listen to your
problems year round, but you don't want to hear
about ours? The wall between us just came down,
but we can't talk to each other, because one of the
two parties doesn't want to hear about the other? Do
you realize that your conversations with us always
finish the same way? You tell us to piss off when you
run out of arguments, and we're left alone, riled up
and frustrated, because we're facing a bundle of
nerves, who's deaf and dumb and pigheaded!

> *ALBERTINE stands up and goes toward the window.
> She glances at her watch again.*

ÉDOUARD:

> I know you can't leave the living room because
> you're waiting for Alex, so I'll go on talking to you,
> even if you've put on your deaf-dumb-and-blind suit
> of armour! Don't worry … if you really can't hear
> me, I'm the one who'll look ridiculous, but if you're
> just pretending and you're actually listening, maybe
> it'll be worth the effort. I say, maybe, because we can
> never be sure about anything with you—

ALBERTINE:

> With me, you can always be sure about one thing:
> bad luck is never far away!

ÉDOUARD:

> Ah ha, you were listening to me.

ALBERTINE:

> I was listening, but I can pull the plug whenever I
> want.

ÉDOUARD:

> Right, and turn everything off, even reality!

> *She turns toward him brusquely.*

ALBERTINE:

> Will you stop saying that?!

ÉDOUARD:

> Not until you change.

ALBERTINE:

> To listen to the rest of you talk, it's like I live in a
> fantasy world that no one else can see! I see crises
> where there aren't any, I suspect things that don't
> exist, I make up problems you can't see! I don't have
> enough imagination for that, Édouard, I've told you

63

that a hundred times! I've got no imagination! I leave that to the rest of you. Every one of you has enough to go around!

ÉDOUARD:

Now that's not true! You've got more imagination than all of us put together!

ALBERTINE:

That's ridiculous.

ÉDOUARD:

You've just put your finger right on it: your wild imagination—that's your problem!

ALBERTINE:

You really don't want to understand, do you?!

ÉDOUARD:

Oh, it might not be an artistic imagination. When you imagine something, you don't grab a piece of paper to write it down or draw it, but your imagination is pretty darn impressive! You believe in what you make up so much, and you feel it so intensely, sometimes the rest of us start to believe it, too! Or almost. What happens to you is always more dramatic than what happens to other people. You can't step foot out the door without having a couple of crises to report, and when you tell us about them, you relive them right before our eyes … An actress couldn't do better, because an actress would've learned a script, while you improvise it all in one fell swoop, with real sincerity, as if it really did happen the way you tell it! So imagine when something bad does happen! Manna from heaven! Nobody in the family said that what happened with Alex wasn't dramatic, and we were all, even Madeleine, we were all prepared to feel sorry for you, to console you, to try to help you through it, but it wasn't long before we realized that you didn't want to be helped. You were in your element, you were happy like that, and we finally got fed up with your endless scenes! Suffering is all right, it happens to everyone, but at some point it has to come to an end! And with you, because of your boundless imagination—don't tell us you don't have any, it's like denying Mount Royal's in the middle of the city—there's no end to it. It goes on and on.

ALBERTINE:

Quite a picture you paint. Congratulations. If that's what you think of me, it's very revealing. If I understand correctly, and please let me know if my imagination is misleading me, nothing ever happens to me that's of any importance to the rest of you. Everything I feel is insignificant, you could cross out my existence and forget me within a couple of days! If I'd never been born, it would make no difference. And I exaggerate everything, to make myself seem important! Is that it? That's the only way I can attract your attention? By making up crises that don't exist?

ÉDOUARD:

It's true, Bertine, your imagination gets the best of you … Take away seventy-five per cent of what you just said there … I'm not saying I think you want to attract attention, not at all … Don't add paranoia to all your other faults! (*more gently*) Listen to me … just listen a bit longer … When you're lying in your bed, and you've been crying for hours, wringing

your sheets, exhausted from not being able to sleep
… don't you … I don't know … don't you get some
kind of pleasure out of what you feel? Aren't you …
a bit … happy?

ALBERTINE:

Are you crazy? You must be crazy! You're the one
with an overactive imagination, Édouard, and you
should save it for your life beyond these four walls!
Leave it at the door when you come home! Are you
telling me that I enjoy suffering? *Are you telling me
that I enjoy suffering?* When I'm lying there in my bed,
like you say, and I'm exhausted from crying, don't
you think I'd like to be able to stop? Don't you think
I'd like to be able to sleep like everyone else? It's
easy to accuse me of enjoying it. But when you've
got no strength left, Édouard, has that ever
happened to you, having no strength left? When
you've got no strength left, when you're at your wits'
end, and you're dying to fall asleep and forget
everything, then you feel another one coming on …
another wave, another flood of tears even though
you thought there wasn't a tear left in your body …
when you feel this ball of fire in your belly, burning
so hot you start banging your head against the wall
beside your bed, when you want to take the whole
world and smash it on the wall along with your head,
you want to destroy the whole world just to stop
suffering, what can you do to get through that? Tell
me! What can you do? Instead of just criticizing me,
give me a solution. Okay? If you're so smart! Don't
just say I should shake myself out of it, get up, take a
bath, put on a pretty dress and go out! Going out
seems to work for you, you might be able to forget
everything around here once you walk out the door,

but not me! There's nothing out there for me, except the American Spaghetti House and the movies! And that's not enough to make me forget my bad luck! The movies all have happy endings and the American Spaghetti House is just a way to earn a living! If I didn't have to show up there every morning to feed you, I'd never set foot there again in my life! I'm just a poor twenty-year-old girl, who's too sensitive and too ignorant to understand the complicated things that happen to her and drive her crazy, and you just accused me of enjoying it—

ÉDOUARD:
The scene you're making right this minute is a perfect example of what I mean—

ALBERTINE:
(*outraged*) I enjoy making the scene I'm making now? Is that what you're saying?

*Brief silence.*

ÉDOUARD:
Yes. If you scratch beneath the surface a bit ... if you ask yourself a few questions, if you ask yourself the right questions, you'll realize I'm right, Bertine. That's why I'm telling you to loosen up a bit. Strip off a few layers, forget some of the details, try to de-dramatize all of it, and you'll realize that life isn't that complicated, and that you're not incapable of understanding what's happened to you.

ALBERTINE:
I guess there's no use in our talking about it. Since everything that comes out of my mouth is nothing but crazy ideas and lies. Is that what you're saying?

ÉDOUARD:

It's not lies—

ALBERTINE:

So what is it then? Just crazy ideas ...

ÉDOUARD:

It's not crazy ideas either ... Wait ... I have to find the right words—

ALBERTINE:

You can say that again! You better find the right words or you won't have a tongue to find any, believe me!

ÉDOUARD:

(*quietly*) When some little thing goes wrong for you, Bertine ... a bit of bad luck ... some little thing that doesn't work out ... Let's say you miss your streetcar, and you were already late ... Do you manage to overcome your little setback, to set it right, or do you pounce on it and start imagining how to blow it up, how to exaggerate it, how to tell us about it later, exactly the way you imagined it?

ALBERTINE:

What are you getting at?

ÉDOUARD:

Try ... try to remember ...

ALBERTINE:

I just want to say, we're a far cry from what happened between Alex and me.

ÉDOUARD:

Even that … even what happened between you and Alex … you wearing Madeleine's dress and the fact that you're here waiting for Alex—

ALBERTINE:

I won't have to tell you about it, you'll be my witnesses! That way you'll see for yourselves if I exaggerate!

ÉDOUARD:

But how will you feel about it, Bertine? And how do you feel about it right now? What will be more important, what we see or what you think happened? (*Brief silence.*) You're scraping the bottom of the barrel tonight, Bertine. What will you do afterwards? After the bottom of the barrel, what will be left?

ALBERTINE:

(*on the verge of tears*) The bottom of the barrel, as you say, is all I have left! It's my last chance, Édouard! If I don't do this … Listen, I really believe, *I really believe* that I still have a chance with Alex and I'm going to take it.

ÉDOUARD:

But he's your sister's beau now!

ALBERTINE:

Well, that's a mistake. And I'm going to try to correct it.

ÉDOUARD:

I don't believe you. I think you know very well that you don't have a chance and this will just give you one more reason to—

ALBERTINE:

>(*cutting him off*) Get the hell out of here! Get out of this living room! Damn queer! Can't even lead a normal life, he hangs out with a bunch of faggots and carries on in front of everyone right downtown, and he dares criticize other people and give them advice!

ÉDOUARD:

>(*softly*) Hear me out, Bertine …

ALBERTINE:

>I heard you out! And then some! You're sick! And if I'm sick too, then you're at death's door. I don't know how I'll be able to look you in the eye tomorrow, and the day after tomorrow, and all the days to come. I don't know how I'll manage to eat my mashed potatoes and my peas across the table from you. For years to come! Because I'm not about to get married, that's clear, and you, you're tied to your mother's apron strings, that's even clearer. If I don't speak to you at the supper table, Édouard, don't you speak to me either!

ÉDOUARD:

>You see … just listen to what you're saying … Listen to what you just said … Listen to the drama you just cooked up … You're already dragging this out for years to come … You're imagining how bad you'll feel about it tomorrow, the day after tomorrow, then, what, in ten, twenty years? You won't speak to me at the supper table for the next twenty years? That's so ridiculous! (*very low*) On the one hand, you think you're going to win back Alex by wearing Madeleine's dress, and on the other, you're predicting that you'll remain an old maid and you

won't speak to me for years! Make up your mind!
You enjoy it, Bertine, that's the problem. That's how
it's always been, and how it always will be!

*She slaps him.*

ALBERTINE:
That's the only answer you deserve!

ÉDOUARD:
A slap in the face is no argument, Bertine.

ALBERTINE:
It's the best argument. Because it expresses
contempt.

ÉDOUARD:
Is that it? Is the scene over?

ALBERTINE:
As far as I'm concerned, it never took place!

ÉDOUARD:
Well, we know that's not true.

*He heads for the door slowly.*

ÉDOUARD:
You'll relive it in your mind, you'll dwell on it, you'll
transform it, improve it, make it crueller, to make it
more interesting, and when you bring it up,
probably with Ma, it will have taken on its real shape
in your head, its real meaning, another stroke of bad
luck, another reason to complain about life in
general, and me in particular. Another beautiful
jewel in your crown of thorns.

*He turns back to her, before exiting.*

ÉDOUARD:

I won't mind eating my mashed potatoes and my peas sitting across the table from you for years to come, I'll have a clean conscience. In the meantime, you can tell Ma the queer went to strut his stuff down Saint Catherine Street ... to cleanse himself of this rotten mess ...

*He exits. ALBERTINE goes back to sit on the sofa. Lights up another cigarette.*

ALBERTINE:

Nobody's going to prevent me from going all the way. Because I know I'm right!

*ALEX appears in the doorway. He notices her almost immediately, hesitates, then starts to retreat.*

ALBERTINE:

Evening, Alex.

ALEX:

Evening, Albertine. Did you hear me come in?

ALBERTINE:

No. Your after-shave gave you away again.

ALEX:

My god, I must smell strong! Did I put on too much?

ALBERTINE:

(*with a sad smile*) No more than usual.

ALEX:

Does that mean I always smell too strong?

ALBERTINE:

No, of course not.

*She stands up to greet him. She's suddenly another woman, lively, light, almost luminous.*

ALBERTINE:

Would you like to take your coat off? You must be dying of the heat with that on.

ALEX:

No, thanks, I've just come to ...

*He stops in the middle of his sentence and blushes.*

ALBERTINE:

It might take a while. She didn't have time to change when she got back from work.

ALEX:

Oh, I see ...

ALBERTINE:

So you may as well make yourself comfortable ... Give me your coat, have a seat on the sofa.

ALEX:

You must understand that I don't feel comfortable—

ALBERTINE:

Why not? C'mon, Alex, we have to put all that behind us.

ALEX:

Oh, really? Well, I'm relieved ...

ALBERTINE:

Let bygones be bygones, we have to move ahead ...

ALEX:

It's just that I heard ... I mean ...

ALBERTINE:

> You're still so handsome when you blush ...

*ALEX squirms with embarrassment.*

ALBERTINE:

> Strange, you're not usually the shy type ... Good
> heavens, Alex, if you go on blushing, you going to
> explode! Fan yourself a bit, do something, you look
> like you're going to faint!

*She laughs ... a peal of false laughter, too theatrical.*

ALBERTINE:

> Can I get you something to drink? I'd love to offer
> you a beer, but, as you know, my mother refuses to
> keep any alcohol in the house ... and that's why my
> father spends his days at the tavern ...

ALEX:

> No, no, thanks. I'm not thirsty.

ALBERTINE:

> Not even a little glass of water?

ALEX:

> No, no, thanks. I'm not thirsty.

ALBERTINE:

> (*laughing*) Good heavens, a real parrot!

> *She goes on laughing. He obviously doesn't know
> what to do with himself.*

ALBERTINE:

> Strange, you don't have the reputation of being shy
> with girls ...

ALEX:

It's different with you.

ALBERTINE:

Why would you suddenly feel shy? I don't understand. You must be hot, take off your coat.

*He hands her his coat, which she puts down on the only armchair where he could have taken refuge, and shows him to the sofa.*

ALBERTINE:

You remember the sofa …

*He sits down, despite himself. She doesn't sit down beside him right away.*

ALBERTINE:

Everything still going well at work?

ALEX:

I've finished training with my father … I'm going out on the road by myself for the first time this fall …

ALBERTINE:

That's great.

ALEX:

My father's giving me some of his customers, even if business is really bad … Like he says himself: "Nobody's buying anything these days, so this will cut back on my mileage."

ALBERTINE:

(*falsely concerned*) Is it true that nobody's buying anything these days?

ALEX:

It's terrible. We've lost about fifty per cent of our business. And lots of people who bought on credit in the past can't afford to pay what they owe us ... And the newspapers say the Depression has only begun.

ALBERTINE:

And you want to get married anyway?

*Tense silence.*

ALEX:

Did Madeleine tell you that?

ALBERTINE:

Yes.

ALEX:

The Depression doesn't eliminate our feelings, Albertine.

ALBERTINE:

That's true.

*She goes to sit down beside him, casually, as if worried about her sister.*

ALBERTINE:

But are you sure you'll be able to support her? You know, I'm her older sister, and I have a responsibility to ask that ... I don't mean to be indiscreet, I hope you realize that ...

ALEX:

(*defensively*) Yes, yes, I know. But don't worry, Albertine, I'd never marry a woman if I wasn't sure I could support her.

ALBERTINE:

    Has she said yes?

ALEX:

    I haven't asked for her hand officially yet … I mean, I haven't spoken to your father … But she, yes, she said yes, but we don't know what he'll say.

ALBERTINE:

    You know that Pa really listens to me … A lot of things around here go through me before reaching him …

ALEX:

    Oh, really?

ALBERTINE:

    You don't remember?

ALEX:

    I never had that much to do with him.

ALBERTINE:

    That's true, you never reached that point with me …

       *ALEX doesn't know how to react.*

ALBERTINE:

    You might do better to wait till the Depression is over.

ALEX:

    It can go on for years—

ALBERTINE:

    And you can't wait for years …

ALEX:

(*after a brief hesitation*) No, neither one of us can ...
We'll live with my father until I've saved enough to
find an apartment that suits us ... We'd really like to
move up near Mount Royal Ave.

ALBERTINE:

Does she know that?

ALEX:

What? Moving near Mount Royal? Yes, and she's
happy to get away from here ...

ALBERTINE:

No, I meant that you're going to live with your
father ...

ALEX:

Of course.

ALBERTINE:

Oh, really ... and she doesn't mind?

ALEX:

Doesn't seem to.

ALBERTINE:

Well, I'll be ...

*She's beginning to be visibly nervous. She stands up.*

ALBERTINE:

Do you mind if I smoke?

ALEX:

I thought you were supposed to stop?

*She turns to look at him.*

ALBERTINE:

If someone had asked for my hand, I might have stopped ...

ALEX:

Listen, Albertine, I'm not comfortable with this conversation ...

ALBERTINE:

No need to say that, Alex, it's obvious. And I fully understand. It won't take long, don't worry ... It might hurt a bit, but it won't take long.

ALEX:

You were waiting for me, weren't you? I should've known. If you're looking for an explanation, I'm not prepared yet ...

ALBERTINE:

You need a lot of preparation.

ALEX:

It takes time before you can talk about these things.

ALBERTINE:

You're much quicker when you want to woo the girls ...

ALEX:

I don't want to woo the girls, I woo one girl at a time ...

ALBERTINE:

That's not what they say about travelling salesmen ...

ALEX:

When you want to sell something to a housewife in the back of beyond, it's perfectly normal to use a few

compliments … But why should I talk about this
with you, I don't owe you any explanations …

*He realizes too late what he has just said.*

ALBERTINE:
Don't you?

*She goes back to sit down beside him.*

ALBERTINE:
Why did you take off like you did, Alex? I got a letter
from Papineauville, saying it was all over, that's it.
And I never saw you again until you started going
out with my sister, and even then, only from afar,
because I avoided you as much as you avoided me.
Around here, they say it's because I scared you off. Is
that true? Did I really scare you, Alex?

ALEX:
I told you I'm not prepared—

ALBERTINE:
Make an effort. I wasn't prepared when I got your
damn letter, but I had to take it anyway …

*He stands up.*

ALBERTINE:
Don't tell me you're going to leave without
answering such a simple question?

ALEX:
The question is simple, the answer isn't.

ALBERTINE:
(*whose aggressiveness has returned*) Well, use your
salesman's gift for gab and make up a nice one for
me, you can do it! Pretend I'm a housewife in the

back of beyond and you want to sell me something I don't need.

ALEX:
You know very well, Albertine, that I'd never say just any old thing to you ... I'd like to be able to say the right thing, but I'm not sure I can ...

*ALBERTINE starts to wipe the tears she's trying to hold back.*

ALBERTINE:
Why did you dump me like that, Alex, why? I was so hurt! I still am! Really! If you only knew! But you probably do. Somebody must've gone and squealed to you, describing everything right down to the last detail. Is it true that I scared you off? I just want to know if it's true that I scared you that bad ...

ALEX:
(*after a long silence*) Sometimes we don't realize the effect we have on people ... We think we're all right, we think we're doing the right things, and in the long run, it turns out that's not what people expected from us ...

ALBERTINE:
I didn't do the right things? Which things, Alex, which things?

ALEX:
At first, it was just little things, nothing important ... I don't know how to put it ... I'm afraid you'll find it stupid and you won't understand what I mean ...

ALBERTINE:

I'm listening, Alex, I've never wanted to understand something so bad in my whole life, so don't hold back ...

ALEX:

Actually, you can be pretty suffocating, Albertine, and I don't think you realize it.

ALBERTINE:

Suffocating?

ALEX:

It begins with little things, like I said ... Look, it's hard to explain, because each thing is no big deal in itself, but when you put them together ... it's the accumulation that adds up and becomes unbearable ... And after a while, when all those things are there ... how can I put it, when you've set them up, patiently, one by one—those little things might be insignificant but there are so many of them, suddenly there's nowhere left for a man to go, he's got no freedom, he can't breathe, you are everywhere ...

ALBERTINE:

I prevented you from breathing!

ALEX:

Oh yes ... And when a man realizes he can't breathe anymore, that he has nowhere to go, no more freedom, because you are everywhere, Albertine, everywhere, there's no escape! And not only have you invaded everything, but before we know it, you're making plans for the future, you think it will go on forever, you're planning to cling to us and prevent us from breathing till our dying day! And you have the nerve to call that love!

ALBERTINE:

It is love!

ALEX:

It's not love, Albertine, it's selfishness.

ALBERTINE:

Selfishness! So now I'm selfish! I'm selfish!

ALEX:

I knew you didn't realize it. Selfish people never realize that they're selfish, and the person who points it out to them is always the worst monster! Well, I'm ready to play the role of worst monster—yes, Albertine, you are selfish.

ALBERTINE:

Everything I did was for you ...

ALEX:

Everything you did was for *you*, Albertine, for your own welfare, for your own future. You fed off my energy! I was the object of your love, but it could have been anyone else, what mattered to you was that you were in love. Or that you believed you were!

ALBERTINE:

How can you say something horrible like that! I only thought of you. I never thought of anything or anyone else! Never.

ALEX:

That's the problem, Albertine, I never asked for that.

ALBERTINE:

You didn't want me to love you!

ALEX:

That's not what I'm saying! I didn't want you to love
me like that …

ALBERTINE:

I don't understand, Alex, I swear I don't understand
… You wanted me to love you less?

ALEX:

Differently … It was … it was too intense all the
time! We can't always be intense like that, it's
impossible. When we went to the movies, you
expected me to look at you, not the screen, like you
were jealous of the movie we were watching!

ALBERTINE:

But that's what I did, Alex …

ALEX:

I know, you were always looking at me to see how I'd
react, you'd spend the evening turning your head
constantly, and it got on my nerves, you have no
idea …

ALBERTINE:

Why didn't you tell me?

ALEX:

I told you hundreds of times! "Albertine, stop
looking at me like that and watch the movie!" Don't
you remember?

> *ALBERTINE registers the blow, she even shifts
> uncomfortably.*

ALEX:

> You see, you don't remember. You only listen when
> you feel like it!

ALBERTINE:

> But it was important for me to know if you liked the
> movie.

ALEX:

> People don't always have to like the same things at
> the same time! When you'd suddenly get a
> headache, in the middle of the movie, was it because
> you thought I didn't like it?

ALBERTINE:

> That's right. I made it up so we could leave, because
> you weren't enjoying yourself … You see, I'm not so
> selfish …

ALEX:

> I'm sorry, but that is selfish. Secretly, deep down
> inside, I bet you were proud of yourself for making a
> sacrifice. You probably thought it was admirable to
> deprive yourself of the rest of the movie just because
> I didn't seem to like it. The proof of it is, you never
> asked me. You never asked: "Are you enjoying this,
> Alex? If you're not, we can leave." No, it had to be
> the big sacrifice, right away. Gosh, I'm nice, I'm so
> generous, I love him so much, I give up so much for
> him! You see, that's just one detail, and I feel stupid
> criticizing you for that because it's not that serious,
> in itself. But I'm not about to start listing off all
> those things, Albertine, just to make you
> understand! I felt trapped! From the moment I set
> foot in here to pick you up, till the moment I
> brought you back to the door, I felt trapped! Not in

the beginning, of course, I was really attracted to you, I thought you were nice, I thought you were funny ... At one point, I thought I had found the right person, too. But suddenly, one evening, I started to see things differently ... because it was too much ... too fast, Albertine, and I felt trapped.

ALBERTINE:

And you don't feel that way with Madeleine?

ALEX:

Madeleine gives me room to breathe. She wasn't the first one to start talking about the future, she wasn't the first one to mention marriage, she never started making references to having kids, to finding a quiet apartment in the east end of the city, and she makes me sit through movies I don't like!

ALBERTINE:

She's smarter than I am, I guess!

ALEX:

She's less demanding, at least.

ALBERTINE:

You were the centre of my life!

ALEX:

That's right, and I was your only chance to get out of here!

ALBERTINE:

Don't tell me you think that's why I loved you!

ALEX:

You didn't love me, Albertine, stop saying that ... I was ... I don't know ... It was more like obsession than love ... You wanted it to work so bad, you wanted so bad to have me just for yourself that it became an obsession, and you lost me, because—it's true, the people who said that were right—I got scared.

ALBERTINE:

And all along ... I thought you liked having me fuss over you like that.

ALEX:

You believed what you wanted to believe.

ALBERTINE:

I thought you liked the fact that I was so passionate. I woke up in the morning thinking of you, I went to work thinking of you, I ate my meals thinking of you ... and I thought you felt the same way ... I used to say to myself, I bet he's thinking of me now, too ... I adore my father, everyone tells me I shouldn't because they don't respect him, but what I feel for my father is nothing compared to how I worshipped you.

ALEX:

You should've worshipped me less and loved me more ...

ALBERTINE:

I couldn't, Alex! You don't realize the place you occupied in my life. You even took my father's place! I could have devoted the rest of my life to you! The rest of my life! I wouldn't have noticed anything else! I wouldn't have noticed anything except the children we had together and the way you cared for me, and the life you provided me with! Nothing else!

ALEX:

And what about me in all that?

ALBERTINE:

I was sure I could change because of you, I was sure I could correct my faults, my moods, my temper, if I devoted my life to you.

ALEX:

And you thought I'd let you take over?

ALBERTINE:

I'm not a good person, Alex, but I thought I could become one thanks to you.

ALEX:

At my expense? Albertine, you're not listening to me! You wanted to do all that at my expense.

ALBERTINE:

I thought, for a while, I'd met someone who finally understood me. I even went on dreaming after I got your letter, during my nervous breakdown ... During my temper tantrums, I thought if only I could talk to him, explain how much I love him, he'll understand, he'll come back, but you're like all the others, the more I talk to you, the more I explain, the more you insist that it isn't love ... That's what they say, too ... I didn't love you ... Even Pa told me that once!

ALEX:

And you think you're right, everyone else is wrong?

ALBERTINE:

Yes. That's what love is for me.

ALEX:

Well, I hope you'll meet someone who's able to appreciate it, as you say. I'm sure there's someone, somewhere, who wants nothing more and who's waiting for you …

*He picks up his coat.*

ALEX:

Tell Madeleine I'll wait for her at the restaurant.

ALBERTINE:

You can't stand being here anymore?. You feel trapped?

ALEX:

Yes.

*He heads for the door.*

ALBERTINE:

Don't leave, Alex. Not right away. Not yet.

ALEX:

I think we've said everything we had to say to each other …

ALBERTINE:

No! I would have things to say to you till the day I die … I'd never get fed up, I'd never get tired—

ALEX:

That's where you're wrong, Albertine. One fine day, you'd realize that your beautiful, passionate love wasn't what it used to be, then, slowly but surely, like all passion—

ALBERTINE:

That's not true! My passion will never fade!

ALEX:

> Oh, yes, it is true. No passion lasts for a lifetime,
> Albertine …

ALBERTINE:

> So why are you marrying Madeleine, then, if passion
> can't last a lifetime?

ALEX:

> I never used the word passion.

ALBERTINE:

> You don't love my sister passionately?

ALEX:

> No.

ALBERTINE:

> And you're marrying her anyway?

ALEX:

> Yes. It's apt to last longer.

ALBERTINE:

> And I suppose you didn't love me passionately
> either?

ALEX:

> No, I didn't.

ALBERTINE:

> And what if it happens to you, some day? What if
> you suddenly fall passionately in love with someone?

ALEX:

> I don't think it will ever happen. But if it does, I'll
> deal with it then. In the meantime, I'm not going to
> refuse to make a life for myself, just in case I find
> passion some day. What if I don't find it till I'm

sixty? I will have wasted my youth! I want a wife and kids, even if they're not born of passion. Passion is made for people like you, Albertine. People who refuse to compromise. Who believe that falling in love means taking possession of another person's life. And those people are impossible to live with! I don't intend to possess anyone, or let myself be possessed by anyone either. Not by you, or by Madeleine ... And I know I have a better chance with Madeleine than with you, so ... You'll grow older, Albertine, and you'll finally understand what I mean.

> *He walks towards the door.*

ALEX:

A few years from now, when you're married with kids in an apartment in the east end of the city, we'll be able to laugh about this. At least, I really hope we can. For your sake. And I'll just be your brother-in-law, and in time, you won't even notice me anymore ...

ALBERTINE:

Don't leave! Please don't leave! Once you're gone, there'll be no hope left! There'll be no hope of anything, do you understand what that means? It can't be true! It's impossible! Do you know what you're doing to me? Do you? If you marry my sister, I'll have to put up with the two of you, with your happiness, with your children, every day of my life for the rest of my life. Because you'll be right there. We won't be able to avoid each other! Do you realize what that means? What that means for me? Every day of my life will bring pain, a reminder of my unhappiness. Every day will bring unhappiness, Alex, because of you!

*He exits.*

ALBERTINE:

(*shouting*) In the meantime, don't expect me to go to your wedding!

*ALBERTINE collapses on the sofa. But she isn't crying. VICTOIRE appears in the doorway.*

ALBERTINE:

You listened to everything, didn't you?

VICTOIRE:

I didn't listen, I heard.

ALBERTINE:

What's the difference?

VICTOIRE:

You were talking loud enough for me to hear bits and pieces. I didn't hear everything.

ALBERTINE:

But enough to give you a good idea? Enough to judge me? Enough to blame me, again?

*VICTOIRE goes to sit beside her.*

VICTOIRE:

You're my daughter, Bertine, I don't judge you.

ALBERTINE:

No, that's true, you blame me without judging me, it's much easier! Well, don't try to console me either. I can't be consoled, Ma! I can't be consoled! I just spilled my last tear! I have none left! I'll never cry

again! Never! Over anyone! Not over Alex! Not over
you! Not even over myself!

VICTOIRE:

In time—

ALBERTINE:

Don't you start now! Forget time! In time, I'll
become meaner, ruder, more stubborn, more
pigheaded! You haven't seen anything yet, Ma.

VICTOIRE:

You want to make us pay for your failure?

ALBERTINE:

I'll make you pay for refusing to understand me.

VICTOIRE:

So the whole world should change so things can be
the way you'd like them to be?

ALBERTINE:

Yes.

VICTOIRE:

I can't say I don't understand you. But that's a road
you have to travel alone. I can't help you, because I
travelled down that road once myself, and once is
enough. Three of my children were a consolation to
me, they consoled me without asking too many
questions, because they loved me, and they could
guess, from afar, what I'd been through … and they
forgave me, I think … But you … You're going to be
alone with your pain, Bertine. All your life. From
this day on … No one will ever understand you,
you'll refuse to change, and you'll suffer alone in
your corner. This might be the last time we have a

real talk, Bertine. My daughter, my poor little girl, try to make an effort before it's too late.

*VICTOIRE stares at her daughter for a long time, then stands up and exits.*

ALBERTINE:
I'll become like a diamond. A black diamond. Black and hard.

*She lights up a cigarette.*

ALBERTINE:
It's all over before it began.

*She smokes.*

ALBERTINE:
It's all over before it began.


*The End.*